-The Poet In Me

-Lonnie Budro

TotalRecall Publications, Inc.
1103 Middlecreek
Friendswood, Texas 77546
281-992-3131 281-Tel
www.totalrecallpress.com

All rights reserved. Except as permitted under the United States Copyright Act of 1976, No part of this publication may be reproduced, stored in a retrieval system, or transmitted in any form or by any means electronic or mechanical or by photocopying, recording, or otherwise without prior permission of the publisher. Exclusive worldwide content publication / distribution by TotalRecall Publications, Inc.

Copyright © 2023 by -Lonnie Budro
Book Cover Graphics by: Jessica Budro

ISBN: 978-1-64883-3069
UPC: 6-43977-43069-4

FIRST EDITION
1 2 3 4 5 6 7 8 9 10

This is a work of poetry. The characters, names, events, views, and subject matter of this book are either the author's imagination or are used fictitiously. Any similarity or resemblance to any real people, real situations or actual events is purely coincidental and not intended to portray any person, place, or event in a false, disparaging or negative light.

The scanning, uploading and distribution of this book via the Internet or via any other means without the permission of the publisher is illegal and punishable by law. Please purchase only authorized electronic editions, and do not participate in or encourage electronic piracy of copyrighted materials. Your support of the author's rights is appreciated.

Table of Contents

Chapter One: -The Poet In Me 1

- -The Poet In Me 2
- My Poetic Journey 4
- Masterpiece 6
- Haunted 7
- The Pen 8
- I'll Paint You A Picture 10
- The Rain 12
- A Well Written Poem 13
- Regret 14
- Lost In Translation 15
- My poetry 16
- Memories 17
- Interruptions 18
- Seeds 20
- The Best Poem Ever Written 21
- A Poem Is A Piece Of Art 22
- The Choice 23
- If I Never Write Another Poem 24
- Have Mercy 25
- Crossroads 26
- Right Here 27
- Where do I Fit In? 28
- Poetry Is Easy 30
- I Don't Read Poetry 32
- True Love 33
- I Met A Poet 34
- There Is A Poet In Me 35
- I Didn't Know 36
- Insanity 38
- Awoke 39
- Sister 40
- My Job 42
- Respect 44
- Take my hand 45
- Memory Lane 46
- A Mother 47

Approval?..49
The War Of Art...50
The Battle..52
The Wand...53
A Letter..54
RIP Charlie Daniels..55
The Shoreline..56
A Cool Fall Night...57
Among My Peers..58
A Rhyme In A Line..59
What To Do?...60
The Title for Our Poem..62
It's Not A Competition...64
Wordsmith...65
Haters Gonna Hate..66
A Gifted Poet..68
A Rare Exception..69
Do What Is Right..70
For Only Me..71
From My Front Porch..72
In That Place...73
I felt Like Writing...74
I took A Break...76
Interpret This..77
When The Poet Goes Away..78
There With You..79
What I Want..80
When I Write...81
You Were Here...82
My Shepherd...83
Poetry Of Old..84
The Shot...85

Chapter Two: Difficult Poetry to Write 86

A Trail I've Taken...87
The hardest words to rhyme...88
Me..90
Convictus..91
a·be·ce·dar·i·an..92
Double a·be·ce·dar·i·an...94

Chapter Three: Addiction 96
- Addiction 97
- The Wolf 98
- Quitting Meth 99
- The Devil In Me 100

Chapter Four: Funeral Poems 102
- Momma's "Dash" 103
- A Day 104
- Hello 106
- A Songbirds Dream 107
- Why? 108
- Torn In Two 109
- My Love For You (Alzheimer's) 110
- Do not stand at my grave and cry 111
- Glory 112
- The Kingdom 113
- No Dispute 114
- Goodbye 115
- Jacob's Ladder 116
- A Quarter On A Tombstone 118
- Heaven Needs Children Too 119

Chapter Five: What Makes A Poem 120
- Poetry Tip 121
- Poetry Tip II 122
- Poetry Tip III 123
- Whataburger 124
- Whataburger (Poem #2) 125

Chapter One:
-The Poet In Me

-The Poet In Me

Some people call me a poet
And I don't want to say it's a lie
Because there is a poet inside of me
But I am not he
Nor he I

You see,

I have heard what this poet has written
I've felt the sting of his tear in my eye
So the -poet in me, and I cannot agree
That I could be he
Or he I

I have seen more than my share of failure
Wiped the sweat, from another failed hope
Had my dreams dashed, right before me
And felt despair every time I was broke

To tell the truth, it's been quite a struggle
What would you do if you're in my place?
When the -poet in me, asks that I set him free
But I'm afraid of the failure we'd face

I have seen many people with talent
Some of whom, have extraordinary skill
And I've taken a look, at this poet in me
And I am afraid that is just how I feel

It is the poet in me who has courage
For without him, I won't even try
So to tell you the truth, there is a poet in me
But I am not he
Nor he I

My Poetic Journey

After my father died many years ago
A picture had been sent to me
It came in a large manila envelope
These were the things that I could see

It was of me, and of my four brothers
And my oldest brothers oldest son
Where we were carrying the casket of our father
And we all loved him, ... everyone

That picture impacted me immensely
I remembered the pain of what we had done
And I sat down and wrote my very 1st poem
And I decided to call it "A Father's Son"

I hadn't ever even tried to write a poem
But I remembered "Mary had a little lamb"
So I was frightened by what I had discovered
And I locked it away and the door was slammed

And then I lost an aunt, and then another
And some others whom I really had loved
And each time that I unlocked that door
I didn't even have to give him a nudge

It has been just absolutely amazing
What in the hell do I have inside?
I can suddenly write the most beautiful of poetry
Where before I hadn't even ever tried

I promise you that I am not lying
And it's getting harder to keep him contained
You have no ideal of the struggle
And I need someone to help me to explain

"WHY ME?" I've asked God in prayer
And then the devil in me wants to come out
And then there's a battle of Good Vs Evil
And sometimes it turns into quite a bout

"To the Victor, goes the spoils" We've all heard this
And I don't even want to hear your 'Holier than thou"
You need to walk a day inside these shoes
And I guarantee that you won't feel so proud

I see things that are ugly all around me
And the poet I have inside me wants to vent
But I don't want to use this gift for evil
When I believe inside my heart it's heaven sent

So please try not to be very judgmental
I'm just trying to explain so you can see
Sometimes I might sign a poem using -Lonnie
And then sometimes it's (the poet in me)

Masterpiece

I may never write the masterpiece
You sometimes see inside a frame,
For the words I write are simple
And are not meant to lead to fame

The poet who lives inside of me
Must breathe to stay alive,
So I set him free, from time to time
And he opens up my eyes

Where once, I had been blinded
But now, I somehow see,
What an extraordinary gift he had
And has put inside of me

I do not feel that I am worthy
How many times Lord, have I prayed?
The gift you put inside of me
Still leaves my heart, afraid

Then He told me in a whisper
"For the sake, of a single soul,
You write what you are given.
And they'll know I told you so "

So I write the words, I listen
He makes tangible the pain,
The poet, can tell 'The Story'
That I never could explain

So when he's finally finished
And his soul is put at peace,
Whatever the poet wrote that day
Becomes my masterpiece

Haunted

I held tighter to my pillow as the fog began to clear
This dream seemed never ending, as I felt somebody near
In the early morning darkness; just before the dawning day
On a path made of cobblestone, we walked along the way

Tree branches almost empty, reaching out to us like claws
Somewhere in the distance; I could swear I heard applause
My silent companion walked along, while covered by a hood
A gentle breeze, swept the leaves, where once a poet stood

Iron gates with broken hinges had appeared just up ahead
The moss covered sign above them, introduced us to the dead
But just before we entered, my companion raised his hand
Then he pointed to a place, where he summoned me to stand

An audience had been assembled from among the many stones
Poets came from near and far, to hear what they had longed
I stood there on that well worn spot, alongside of the fence
While silence fell among us, as my reading had commenced

Then I read them several poems; which I have yet to write
As each of them applauded, as they disappeared from sight
Then I pulled the covers closer, as I awoken with a chill
Was this just a dream I had; or was it really real?

The Pen

"Excuse me sir, may I borrow your pen?"
"This pen"? he asked. Held up with a grin,
"I just had a thought that I wanted to save
And if I don't write it down it will go to its grave"

"Are you a poet?" For that was a nice rhyme"
I said, "No, not really. But I try it sometimes"
He lifted his brow when it happened again
Then smiled, and leaned over. And offered his pen

"Good sir" said he. "I see you answer, in jest"
"But I remember a time when I thought I was best,
I could write it all down, and just let it all flow
And let the poet inside me just put on a show"

"But I didn't share it with others, I kept it all to myself
And I saved hundreds of poems in a box on a shelf,
One day in a fire, I lost all I had wrote
And the poet inside me's, heart had been broke"

"All the life" inside that poetry, had died on that day
The gift I had been given slowly ascended away,
The only thing left as proof of my sin
Is this tired old body, and that wonderful pen"

It will take you on journeys that you'll only see
Then write it all down, as the poet in me,
But whatever you've written must be wrote with desire
Good poetry should never be destroyed by a fire"

I looked down at his pen which I held in my hand
as I listened to this story, from this tired old man,
And when he finished speaking and his words were all gone
I slowly looked around me. But I sat there alone

The pen was a gift. But it looked quite a sight
So I scribbled on my hand, and at least it would write,
I set back on our bench after one final look
Then I pulled off its cap, and I opened a book ...

I'll Paint You A Picture

He sat there in his chair
Alongside the lake where he would stare
At the canvas which stood blank before his eyes

He had his paints and brush
But a face filled with disgust
So he turned and asked if I would like to try

But I just took out my pen
For I knew where to begin
And I began to paint for him a scene with just my words

There was a sky I painted blue
And I dabbed here and there a time or two
Until I painted every feather on a flock of birds

Then I painted him the trees
Just as pretty as you please
And every limb with all its leaves that gave us shade

He would read over my shoulder
As I penciled in another boulder
And he mixed his colors to match each stroke I made

It took me just about an hour
As I wrote of distant showers
And I described in great detail just how it felt

But he struggled with his paint
And then he stopped and said "I can't"
As I described the aroma from the bar-b-cue I smelt

Then I tore out my page
when he offered me a wage
For the purchase of the words I wrote that day

For I had painted him a picture
Where no paint could match the mixture
Of all the things the poet who lives inside me had to say

The Rain

The downpour was pounding on that old metal roof
He sat down in his rocker after he took off his boots,
Then he pulled down his wet hat, til it covered his eyes
Then the only time he'd move, was when he'd shoo away flies

He had an old Treeing Walker, on the porch by his feet
And there was always plenty of food in his bowl he could eat,
Momma would call him 'Sugar'. But grandpa called him "Blue"
Granny said "There just ain't no tellin', what they done got into"

She was shelling purple hull peas, into a bowl on her lap
While grandpa just sat there, and just took him a nap,
The sound of distant thunder, and then it rattled the tin
There is not a place on this planet, where I'd rather have been

A Well Written Poem

I love to read a well written poem
And get lost inside its words,
And briefly take a journey
As if it just occurred

And put aside all my worries
And get lost inside a tale,
And let the poet weave his magic
That has put me in a spell

I want to feel the chill if it is raining
I want to feel the fire that is hot,
I want to be surprised by things unexpected
That reminds me of what I have forgot

I want to feel the tear, that's slowly falling
As it itches while it's running down my face
I want to enjoy every word that is written
That has been so carefully put in its place

And when I can see the poem is finally ending
And feel the sadness, that is deep inside my soul
I silently give thanks to this poet
And the gift he gave, that he won't ever know

Regret

When I stand before my Maker
and the balance scales are set,
I hope the good that I have done in life
out weighs what I regret

Those little acts of kindness
as light as they can be,
Have so much that they must overcome
to find some peace for me

Transgressions that weigh so heavy
That number more than I admit,
Dark shadows through my walk in life
that my heart will not forget

A brief reprieve, my soul receives sometimes
when I help someone in need,
Until the thought of things I've done
brings back dark memories

Good deeds are where I find my peace
To right some wrong I've done,
While I try and walk a straighter path
on this new life, that I've begun

Lost In Translation

When written from the heart
From the very first start,
As a poem slowly fills up a page

Filled with desires
And the trials life requires,
To empty a kind soul of its rage

And when your emotions are spent
And you are in peaceful content,
For your pain has been put into words

A little time has gone by
You read them again with a sigh,
And you edit what your heart said occurred

Words that were written with passion
Words that ran tears down your face,
Surrounded by tiny little errors
You now feel, are way out of place

Make certain while checking your grammar
That every I's dotted and T's crossed,
You don't take away from it's meaning
Or the "Spark" of the poem will be lost

My poetry

I follow no meter
I follow no rhyme,
My poetry is freedom
That freedom is mine

If I brake any rules
Those rules should be broke,
There is a poet inside me
Who is finally awoke

Memories

The poet inside me
He'll come and he'll go
When will he appear?
Nobody knows.

Then in the midst of a poem
He'll leave for a while
To gather his thoughts
And remove any smile

Then with tears full of anguish
That stream down my face
The words that are missing
Are put in their place

His heart is aching
From thoughts of the past
Some wished forgotten
And others to last

Memories are not promised
But while they are here
The bad we remember
The good, we hold dear.

Interruptions

I like to sway to the music of a slow country song …
And feel the beat of the rhythm as we're moving along …
And feel the chill in the air on a hot summer day …
And the sound of a child who is busy at play …

I like the freedom to write what I wanted to say …
Without rules or emotions to get in my way …
Just write what I feel and let it all flow …
And by the end if I win I have put on a show …

No pictures are needed to show you the way …
Your memory reminds you from the words that I say …
What was her name for it seems I forgot? …
In the words of a poem you remember a lot …

I miss him so much and I wish he was here …
Just pause for a moment for that memory so dear …
Then remember another and another one still …
And you can stop to cherish what's being revealed …

Some thoughts of anguish are brought back to life ...
For some it's a loved one a husband or wife ...
I pray it's not a child though for some it is true ...
And for those of you the poet in me grieves with you too ...

And then comes the sun and it lights up the day ...
Because the smile of a child made my poem go astray ...
The sun on my face has now dried up the dew ...
While I look for a metaphor that's easy to use ...

Now after some editing and a real quick review ...
After both of the phone calls that you never knew ...
The text messages the horn honk, the knock at the door ...
The poet inside me couldn't take any more ...

So I learned me a lesson while I'm trying to write ...
Some it doesn't bother but others need quite ...
So I am going to quit typing now and lay down my pen ...
And when the poet is ready I will try it again ...

Seeds

We live our lives
And each have tried
To sow some seed on fertile ground

But God alone
Knows what was grown
From those seeds we've cast around

From butterfly wings
Comes *powerful* things
From deep inside each single storm

So those forgave
By He who saves
Is best decided by who's informed

The Best Poem Ever Written

The best poem ever written
Has been written by you,
When you write what you're feeling
While you know, that it's true

The rhyme doesn't matter
Whether good or it's bad,
When you write about happy
Or when you write about sad

And when these words, are all written
And there's a load off your chest,
Or the beauty you have witnessed
Has been released, from your breast

Then you can take out, all of the errors
And some things, you know are true,
Only after the best poem ever written
Has been written by you

A Poem Is A Piece Of Art

A poem is but a piece of art ...
And a poets pen. A brush ...
Where each word paints a picture ...
And where the colors inside can gush ...

Some will burst forth out of passion ...
Some will sling paint out of pain ...
Some will paint tears of adoration ...
Some will leave things unexplained ...

And as the paint is slowly drying ...
And each stroke, came from your heart ...
Although, "Beauty is the the eye of the beholder" ...
You may have just painted, a 'Work of Art' ...

The Choice

Poetry is an art form
Which has a very wide brush,
It can be a thing of beauty
Or can be filled with disgust.

It focuses on that single tear
Poised, to run down your cheek.
It's written in a child's face
Who hasn't had enough to eat.

It's there inside a drop of blood
Slowly soaking in the ground.
You can hear it in the scream
A newborn child has finally found.

The chosen path is yours to choose
Many have chose to make their own.
But whatever path you choose to take
The choice is yours, and yours alone.

If I Never Write Another Poem

If I never write another poem
And this is the last you'll ever hear,
I hope that some of what I've wrote
Is still read down through the years

If for not but for a single soul
A line I've wrote gives someone pause,
And in that single precious moment spent
They're left standing there in awe

For much of what I know I've wrote
Are those things that some'll find,
That were meant to pierce a soul
For they were sent by those Devine

Have Mercy

I took the chain off of his collar

And then I turned that bad boy loose

He stared at me with mixed confusion

But he'd done shown me all the proof

And I ain't gonna hold him back no longer

He's all growed up, and it's time to go

But Lord have mercy, and heaven help me

I believe he's about to put on a show

Crossroads

When you are standing at the crossroads
And you've looked left and you've looked right
And whatever lies behind you, Is no longer left in sight

You cannot see what's up ahead
And you feel like no one cares
There's another direction yet to look
Have you turned to the man upstairs ?

Right Here

My poet pulled up beside me
And then he yelled, "Get In"

He smiled, and revved his engine up
And said "Let's take her for a spin"

So I sat down, and I closed the door
But I began to smile in fear

These are the times, that're hard to find
These times, like these, right here.

Where do I Fit In?

I've been searching for an answer, to a questions from within.
Where, in this world of poetry, does someone like me, fit in?

I lack the higher education, and do not hold a fine degree.
But I see the proof when I turn loose this poet inside of me.

This is not something that I had hoped for.
Or wished that some day, I'd achieve.

It's that when it's there inside my head,
I can write it down with ease.

This is not written out of arrogance.
Or my conscious would call it sin.

So I'm trying to find the answer.
Where in the hell, do I fit in?

I didn't know anything about poetry.
And I didn't care to know as well.

I've lived a life of rough and tough,
And loved the scent from a shotgun shell.

I've hunted everything that's walked or crawled.
And washed their blood from my knife in a creek.

As a country boy raised in southeast Texas,
Poetry was not something someone seeks.

But it was when my daddy died, after I was grown,
That this journey would begin.

And I would like to ask him a question.
"Daddy, where do I fit in?"

Why is it,
I can see more colors now,
And can find that perfect word?

Why is it,
I now can hear the silence,
That I have never heard?

Why can I see a speck of dust,
And the universe, inside?

Why is it I see the truth,
In spite of all the lies?

Daddy,
Please answer me this question,
and don't just stand there with a grin.

I need to know the answer,
Where do I fit in?

Poetry Is Easy

Poetry is easy
When it comes from the heart,
The hardest thing to do
Is to find where to start.

Then you only use the words
You would normally say,
And don't let fear, or a tear
Ever get in your way.

And if you write it out of anger
While it's still on your mind,
There's a whole lot of peace
That you'll probably find.

So it really doesn't matter
If it isn't written real good,
Poetry will let you tell it
Just the way that you should.

Then you can always come back later
When you've finally cooled down,
There may be a mistake in there somewhere
That you'll be glad that you found.

And if you're broken hearted
And you need a good cry?
Then write it down in poetry
With those tears in your eyes.

And you never have to share it
So write it just how you feel,
And you'll have a piece of what's inside you
That your words have made real.

So, poetry is easy
Something anyone can do,
There's a poet who's in me
And there's a poet in you.

I Don't Read Poetry

I don't read poetry
I read between the lines,
That's where I find the story
The poet hopes we find

To tell a tale of love or hate
Or what's gripped inside a soul,
What's hidden in the crevices
The words would have you know

In times of greatest sorrow
In times we're filled with pride,
That moment which took your breath away
Or when someone special ... died

A broken heart that's torn in two
Or has been trampled on the ground,
That smile that goes from ear to ear
When a new love has been found

These are all the things we hope for
The little treasures that we might find,
So I don't read the poetry
I read between the lines

True Love

"You can tear up an iron skillet, with an eggshell"
Grandpa yelled across the room,
Granny said "You'd best, just get on outta here"
And then threatened him with a broom

Grandpa grabbed his hat from off the nail
Smiled, and then headed on out the door,
There was not a person on this planet
Who had ever loved her more

She cooked him breakfast every morning
And watched him work hard every day,
And he'd always stop and listen
To anything she'd have to say

Her flower pots that lined the porch
The bird bath, beneath the tree,
Two hummingbird feeders full of juice
Were things he loved to see

She loved it when he made a fuss
Over things she loved to cook,
The shine of love in both their eyes
Should be stored inside a book

I Met A Poet

One day while on a journey
I saw a poet stare back at me,
As I leaned across a wooden rail
To see what I could see

The shoreline with its grasses green
With a sky that's bright and blue.
The tiny boats so far away
And this poet saw them too

As I walked along that weathered bridge
He matched me step for step,
Then a gentle breeze, an angel sneezed
And he was lost within its depth

But I see him there more often now
On these days that are nice and calm,
Where he pens a poem each time I'm there
Which sounds more like a psalm

There Is A Poet In Me

There is a poet in me, who is filled, with the passion

There is a poet in me, who has felt all of my pain

There is a poet in me, whom, when he takes the notion

Can find the words, that helps me to explain

There is a poet in me, who is bold, beyond my measure

There is a poet in me, who hides inside my soul

There is a poet in me, who is trapped inside a prison

Who is begging me, to please, just let him go

There is a poet in me, who sees beyond the forest

There is a poet in me, who sees what some don't see

There is a poet in me, whom, I know for certain

Would use his voice, in defense of liberty

I Didn't Know

I was a poet, and didn't know it
Til one day I had to show it
And found that the poet who is inside me's pretty good ...

He hid there in the dark
Until something broke his heart
And then I watched him write the words I never could ...

It has really been quite amazing
When he sets my pen a blazing
Where I just sit back while he takes me for a ride ...

So this poet and I agree
I'm not him and he's not me
For I have failed at almost everything I've ever tried ...

So he lives here deep inside
And he no longer wants to hide
And would break his bonds asunder, and be set free ...

But there are bills to be paid
And not a dime he's ever made
So I have given it all over to God on bended knee ...

So many things to be said
That are trapped inside my head
Which the poet who lives inside me wants released ...

Like a rooster who needs to crow
He just wants to put on a show
And some day I know, he'll write his masterpiece ...

So when I have the time
I will try and be more kind
And release his bonds, and set the poet in me free ...

But I always live in fear
One day he'll disappear
When I turn him loose, and he'll not come back to me ...

Insanity

I check myself each and every day to see if I'm insane
I judge the truth by using proof that matches what is claimed

What I see with my own eyes and then I'm told that I am blind
So I check myself like no one else in case I've lost my mind

But when I see I know for certain just what it was I saw
And when I hear the way they spin it I just have to stand in awe

And when I look around me at those who believe their claim
And It is not me the one I see who must have gone insane

Awoke

A poet awoke inside of me
In just a single day,
It took a photograph that broke my heart
And the pain that it conveyed

Each time I held it in my hand
And saw those things you cannot see,
And suddenly I realized
There's a poet inside of me

He cried like a big ol baby
He had tears run down his face,
But the words I saw him write that day
Are still there to prove my case

You will not find a single poem
That has been wrote before that day
There is a poet who lives inside of me
These are the words he has to say

Sister

These words will not do justice
For what I want to say to you,
You've been there for me all my life
With the little things you do

The love you showed me when I was a child
Through many a scrape and blister,
I took it all for granted
Because you were my sister

As years passed by, and both of us
Grew a little older,
With trials to endure, you were always there
To offer me your shoulder

Through all my life's adversities
You've been there through every one,
I feel less like I'm your brother
And more like I'm your son

Many miles are now between us
And our visit's are just a few,
But the cards and calls keep coming
I expect that much from you

Gray hairs are growing abundant
And now I'm called "sir" or "mister"
I wish everyone had someone, like you
That they could call their sister

To: Margaret

My Job

The alarm goes off at five am
So I get out of bed,
For ten hours I will work today
To keep my family fed

My wife is up to see me off
With a kiss we say goodbye,
I never doubt her love for me
I see it in her eyes

The drive takes forty minutes
It's the time that I reflect,
On all that God has given me
And his blessing I collect

Or home, our cars, our way of life
As modest as they may be,
I don't ever want to take for granted
The things he's done for me

The kids are already home from school
When I walk in the door,
I provide for them the best I can
But they are always wanting more

As a father I accept this life
Though the rewards seem very few,
But it's because I love my family
That I do the things I do

Respect

Daddy said ...

"Pull over,
and you boys, take your hat off.

There comes a line of cars,
With all their headlights on.

And it don't make a damn,
If we don't know em.

You always show respect,
For those that's gone."

Take my hand

Hold my hand and take a walk with me
And just say what's on your mind
We'll stroll along an autumn trail
Where colored leaves are all we find

We'll feel the chill that's in the air
Until our nose begins to sting
And hear the sound of distant geese
And the single cord they sing

So hold my hand, and take this walk with me
And blow your breath into the air
Where we'll watch the wind take it away
Until we both just stop and stare

I am whomever you need me to be
So just reach out, and take my hand
And say those things you need to say
And just know. I understand

Memory Lane

I took a stroll down memory lane
I shed some tears
I felt some pain

I miss your laugh
I miss your touch
I miss the past we loved so much

But now it's gone
And so are you
I'm left with what once was true

I cannot hide
I cannot heal
What's felt inside I know is real

These memories hurt
These memories stain
These memories pave my memory lane

A Mother

Your kiss has healed our bruises
And your hugs have helped us sleep
In the early morning hour
Always the first one on your feet

So many acts of kindness
The selfless labor of your love
God sure knew what he was doing
When he made his plans above

You are the Greatest of his creation
Through You he gives us life
All your tenderhearted compassion
Helps us overcome our strife

And when the day is finally over
And prayers go out to one another
With a gentle kiss, we rest in peace
Thanks too a loving Mother

Poet master

I do not want the words "Poet Master"
To ever appear beside my name.
And I know that some of you are curious,
And would want me to explain.

So for those who know the story,
Of "The poet inside of me"
Through his eyes, there's no disguise,
What he would have you see.

"How do you master what cannot be mastered?
How do you tame, what cannot be tamed?
When you stand in the doorway of creation,
Can what you have beheld, be explained?

A gifted painter can paint many details,
And a talented sculptor, can carve it from stone.
A good musician can play us a nice melody,
But the "Poet"? Well, he stands there alone.

In Battle, he becomes a great warrior.
In Death. He's there to hold onto your hand.
He'll find you peace, in all kinds of trouble.
And help you accept things, you don't understand.

This is not something that someone can master.
"A Rookie" is what I'd much rather be.
I don't ever want to be known as a "Poet Master"
I'm fine with just -The poet in me.

Approval?

I do not write to seek approval
I just need somewhere to vent,
A place to focus all my anger
Until the fire inside is spent

Or when my heart is filled with anguish
Then the poet inside me shines,
It is beyond my comprehension
How these words form in my mind

And when a page is filled with my emotions
And the poet has had his say,
I often crumble up that piece of paper
And just cast it all away

The War Of Art

We all like to see,
a thing of beauty,
And all of us enjoy
our favorite song

Those who love to dance
to the music,
Where you know the words
and have to sing along

But it's the poet
who can take you on a journey,
Somewhere to a place,
that's back in time

Where a memory
that longs to be written,
Is released from all the thoughts
that come to mind

Then are chiseled
into the strongest block of granite,
And then are stored
inside a readers mind

Beauty,
is in the eye of the beholder,
Where poetry,
becomes a painting you cannot find

The Battle

I watched a fight between two angels in a dream while I had slept
One had made an offer for my soul in which the other would not accept,
The first wore clothes in tatters while a sword adorned his hip
And his saliva hissed like acid from between two smiling lips

I never heard the price he offered for the purchase of my soul
The other angel simply drew his sword and told the other "No"
Who brandished then his weapon and the two then crossed their blades
My defender boldly looked him in the eyes and said "He has been Saved"

I stood in sheer amazement as this took place before my eyes
I watched a battle for my salvation and how hard each angel tried,
The fight went on for hours which had then turned into days
Gods angel drew his power from the prayers that people prayed

But it was hate which fueled the other and his strength had been made strong
By a world so full of anger to where no one could get along,
My valiant angel faltered and then that was all it took
My wounded warrior turned to me and said to "Take a look"

There stood ten thousand angels and I saw ten thousand more
What remained of his opponent I just couldn't say for sure,
"It was 'Faith', which brought them here today." This angel said to me
"Now you write what you have witnessed for the whole wide world to see"

The Wand...

Jack and Jill went up a hill
Where Mary, had a little lamb,
Travis brought his dog Old Yeller
His brother Arliss, brought Savage Sam

Then Huckleberry Finn came walking by
And Tom Sawyer, had tagged along,
While little Miss Muffet, sat on a tuffet
Jimmy Hendrix played us a song

Humpty Dumpty sat on a wall
The seven dwarfs, sat on the ground,
Barney Fife fired his gun into the air
And announced "Waldo", has been found"!

Jack be nimble, Jack be quick
But the itsy bitsy spider, won the race,
And the wheels on the bus go round and round ...
Whenever I see your smiling face

So lets go back, to the future
To infinity and beyond,
Where Mary had a little lamb
And Harry Potter, had a wand

A Letter

My friend received a letter
After his daughter had died
Teardrops stained the pages
A grateful mother, had cried

Her son in need of a kidney
Or else he would have died
All hope was lost, she said
Family said their goodbyes

Their miracle, then happened
When a sad tragedy occurred
Some prayers went unanswered
Some prayers, had been heard

RIP Charlie Daniels

"The devil went down to Georgia"
But he tucked his tail and ran
I heard that song ten thousand times
Before I became a man

A "Long haired country boy"
Who grew up in the South
Loved to hear him play his fiddle
And the words out of his mouth

"The legend of Wooley Swamp"
Raised the hair on the back of my neck
"Still in Saigon", and "In America"
Were songs that taught us all respect

Thank you for all the memories
And the songs that helped me through
And the Patriotic Spirit you showed
For our beautiful ... red white and blue.

The Shoreline

It's four thirty in the morning
And I'm standing here alone,
The gentle waves are slowly crashing
Relieving the troubles I have at home

The vast expanse of the silent ocean
The gentle breeze felt on my face,
I close my eyes to hear the whispers
Being released from every wave

The soft sand absorbs my worries
The cool water tugs each one away,
While standing barefoot on the shoreline
Watching the dawning of the day

A Cool Fall Night

It's three a.m. on a cool fall morning
As I sit on the wooden steps of my porch
The sky is filled with a thousand starlight's
The twinkling flames of a far away torch

A lone dog, who barks in the distance
Is quickly answered by those of his kind
These are the fond memories of a poet
That are stored in the back of his mind

The crickets all sing their song in unison
A drop of dew drips, from the metal roof overhead
The moons light has brightened up the darkness
There is a rhythm to what the night has said

Everything else is lost in the silence
Neighborhood toils have all been put to sleep
These are the things that dreams are made of
As out there somewhere, somebody weeps

Among My Peers

I humbly stand here, before my peers,
who have felt, this self same pain.
Who use their words, as best they can.
To try and help themselves, explain.

Thoses who bleed, the same blood I bleed.
Those who have cried, over someone lost.
Who feel they've paid, the ultimate price.
And wonder how much more, will it cost?

I humbly stand here, before my peers,
Who have felt, this self same pain.
Who use their words, as best they can.
To try and help themselves, explain.

A Rhyme In A Line

When you see a rhyme in a line for the very first time,
You'll know that it's true that two is harder to do,

But three you'll agree is much harder to see
When four takes the floor and will not be ignored,

But when five comes alive and cannot be denied
Six does some tricks with a hand full of sticks

Then seven through eleven are whisked off to heaven
While eight's at the gate and is having to wait

But nine's doing fine when it comes to a crime
Then ten gets the win with a grin on his chin

What To Do?

What would you do,
If you could write it like me?
And make it sound so simple,
Until it's easy to read?

And as you tell it to others,
Using plain simple words.
Until not even a poem,
Is what they had heard?

Would you write of religion,
And share the faith that's inside?
And would you tell of the visions,
That you've been trying to hide?

Or maybe write of your past,
And of the things you have felt.
Until you can smell the aroma,
That as a child, you had smelt?

Or would you write books for children,
That could teach as they rhyme.
The ones that a good teacher,
Has been trying to find?

So if you're given this gift,
And you could write it at will.
And any thought, you had imagined,
Your words could make real.
Would you stand up and start shouting
And say "Hey world, look at me?"
Because, that's not the way,
I was raised up to be.

So I'll just write what I'm feeling,
And sometimes share, one or two.
For I have written poems for others,
And I have wrote some, for you.

So there's no need to comment
No one else needs to know.
Whenever my poem touches others
It is felt in my soul.

The Title for Our Poem

When you struggle to find a title
For a poem you need to write,
And what's bottled up inside you
Has got you *spoilin' for a fight

And you're waiting to just get started
Because you don't know what to say?
Then you just hold off, on that title
And get to writin' it, anyway.

And while on this roller coaster of emotions
That we're about to put down on page,
These words that'll tell our story
Filled with our love and with our rage

This thing might change directions
And veer a little bit off the track,
And that there title that we started with
Done come off somewhere in the back.

Sometimes they may be good for focus
As we walk along some guided path
And they're there to lead us on a journey
We may have imagined from our past

But there's times we must search our soul
And find that place we get to know him
And it's often then, and only then
We'll find the title for our poem.

It's Not A Competition

It is not a competition
To write what's in your soul
And then share it all with others
Whom you may never know

Some may write will eloquence
There are those who choose to rhyme
But it is they who tell a story
Who are the hardest ones to find

What is hidden in the crevasses
Along a long, and bumpy road
Are the memories, we are reminded
That these words have never told

So, it's not a competition
When someone's done their very best
And the ghosts alive inside them
Have all been put to rest

Wordsmith

If you ever do meet a wordsmith
Then please point him out to me,

I wanna have me a real good look
So's I can see what there is to see

You might have to hold him down
Just so I can check behind his ears

Cause I ain't seen no one like that
In about a hunnert and fifty years

Haters Gonna Hate

There are those who express kindness
Those who would never berate

There are those who look for goodness
Those who ignore the mistakes

There are those who build up others
Those who will always inflate

There are those who help their brother
Those who'll take a load off his plate

And then ...

There are those who show no kindness
Those who must always berate

There are those who ignore goodness
Those who find every mistake

There are those who tear down others
Those who will only deflate

There are those who burden their brother
Those who'll put more on his plate

So ...

There are those who are the haters
Those who deny something great

And ...

There are those who are much greater
Those who don't reply to their hate

A Gifted Poet

I met a gifted poet
Who could write his words with ease.
And rhyme his lines in perfect time
As pretty as you please.

"What sorcery is this?" I asked him
"How can these things you do, be done?"
As I stepped into his shadow
So he could block me from the sun/son.

He said
"This bright light you see behind me
(As he motioned, with his thumb)
And wherever the light is reaching
Are where my words are from.

You need only step from darkness
And feel the warmth, from whence it came
And accept the words that you are given
Then you yourself, could do the same"

A Rare Exception

She said,
"You are that rare exception
an anomaly I've found.
Who can walk among the shadows
where good poets all abound.

Who can reach inside a broken soul
and feel what some have felt.
And you can paint us all a picture
In every word that you have spelt.

Sometimes, you've given me a tear
but you've also made me smile.
And I often think of things you've said
That I haven't thought of in awhile.

I'm not confused, by the words you use
And you've often given me a lift.
So to me, you are that rare exception
And you have an extraordinary gift"

Do What Is Right

You should do what is right
With all of your might
And let your conscious be your guide.

To uphold what is true
In everything you do
Until the good can no longer hide.

And when you resist what is wrong
By doing good all along
There is something we can all agree.

If we can just avoid the devil
And not get down to his level
Then the bible tells us that he'll flee.

For Only Me

I once wrote a poem
That I won't ever share
For it was written for only me

A poem that don't lie
With tears in my eyes
That I know in my heart, I see

The regrets of my soul
That no one else knows
Those things I wish I'd never done

Then I read it out loud
And I finally felt proud
When I gave it all over to God's Son

From My Front Porch

Sitting on my front porch I see my neighbors
And I like to watch them wave as they go by
Some of them have told me about their troubles
While I sit back and I watch how hard they try

From my front porch I can see the ones who're friendly
And a time or two I've seen some of them cry
Throughout the years I've visited some of their funerals
Because I was there throughout much of their lives

Sitting on my front porch I watch my neighbors
And I like to see them wave as they go by
I hope they're not judging me like I judge them
Those times I ignore the 'beam' that's in my eye

In That Place

When I find me in that place, and then start writing
And every thought that comes to mind, are put to words
Where the poet, who lives deep down inside of me
Can write it down as if it just occurred

It's a time that I'm not worried about the spelling
Are my punctuations all in their right place?
Should I stop for a moment, and contemplate these things
And let the thoughts that were in my mind be erased?

Should I go back now and pretend that I am flawless?
Should I dress up in a set of clothes, I do not wear?
Although many of my words, may be wrote in ignorance
Sometimes that's the way I meant that they be shared

I felt Like Writing

Sometimes when I write, I just feel like writing
And I don't start with a preconceived idea every time
I just sit down here and then it just happens
And most of the time I can make all of it rhyme.

Right off from the start I find me a rhythm
And I try and keep it maintained the best I can
But sometimes something might come along all unexpected
And then I got no choice but to change all of my plans.

But I get a lot of joy after I have read what all I've written
And a lot of the time I am ashamed of what I've wrote
You see, I am a poet who lacks those things of higher education
But I cannot restrain a poet whose bonds have been broke.

the poet in me has breathed the breath of freedom
And must be allowed to say exactly what's on his mind
Poetry restrained, is poetry that is in bondage.
That someone with greater skill could best define.

A songwriter does not need to perform the music
And does not need to be the one who sings the song
As a poet. There are many things which I am lacking.
So I invite someone with the skills, to tag along.

Like a band, who is in need of a drummer
Or a taxi driver, who is in search of a fare
I am a poet who lacks the education
But what I have, I am more than willing to share.

I don't know where I was going when I started writing this.
This poem just grew a little longer as we went.
I just started out, because I felt like writing something.
But now the passion that was inside of me is spent.

I took A Break

I took a break
From all things fake
And turned off my television.

I stopped watching movies
And sounds that are groovy
So I could clear up a lot of my vision.

To find what is real
The things I can feel
And judge by what I see in my heart.

So I sought after truth
And looked for the proof
Of what is tearing our nations apart.

And what I have found
Is that evil abounds
And many of our leaders have led us astray.

But these are the times
Some'll pay for their crimes
And God'll answer prayers that were prayed.

Interpret This

A poem is left to interpretation
While you search inside your soul.
And you alone, knows what is shown
From those memories you know.

Where only you, knows what is true
And your thoughts come back to life.
Be it a smell, a jail, some time in hell.
Or the loss of a child, a friend, a wife.

But sometimes they are beautiful
And you just want to close your eyes.
And step inside, a dream come true
That the poet's poem revives.

That's why it's left to interpretation
Throughout the thoughts that come to mind.
And it is there where we all can share
What a good poem can help us find.

When The Poet Goes Away

My dreams, cannot fill the seams
Whenever the poet in me has gone away.
I'm left with things, and sights unseen
And now I don't know what to say.

Where he's up and gone
And leaves me alone
And he's done this, time and time again.

I need him to stick around
Until all the words are found
And this thing has reached its end

There With You

While watching the twinkle
Of a faraway star.
Oh, how I wonder
How far away you are?

Up above this sky tonight
And all the stars
I see so bright

I wonder if you
Are watching too?
It's when I feel
I'm close to you

What I Want

I want to write
What no one else has written.
I want to say those things
That no one has said.

I want to set free
This thing that lives inside me.
That leaves visions
That dance inside my head.

I want to talk
To those who will listen.
I want to explain
These things that I feel.

I want to share
All of these emotions.
I want my words,
To make all of them real.

I want to hold
These things that I cherish.
I want to share them
With those who're like you.

I want to write
Like no one has written.
I want my words
To make them all come true.

When I Write

Whenever I write
A string draws tight
That life has wrapped around my heart.

It'll tug my pen
And say "begin"
And I'll feel the pain right from the start.

But a brief reprieve
My soul receives
While searching for that proper word.

A thing I've smelt
A touch I've felt
Or an old thought that just occurred.

But then it's back
There is no slack
As this string rips into my flesh

It's times like these
the poet in me sees
And that is when he's at his best

You Were Here

I want to read a poem out loud
One the whole wide world will hear
That comes from within my soul
So I can show them you were here

All the smiles you have left
All the tears you have cried
Those times when we have shared our greatest fear

What you and I've been through
When there was no one else but you
A poem which reminds the world that you were here

My Shepherd

The Lord is my shepherd
No need could be more dear,
He leads me beside still waters
With green pastures growing near

He restores to me my soul again
My cup will overflow,
He leads me in his righteous path
To follow where it goes

When I walk through the valley
And the shadows of death are near,
His rod and staff will comfort me
No evil there I fear

A table he has set for me
Before those who would have me fail,
And in his house, with all his flock
Forever, I will dwell

(Psalm 23)

Poetry Of Old

When I read those poems of long ago
And I find me in that place
Where the words they used, leaves me confused
for we no longer talk that way today

But there's a time that'll come
That this age we're from
Will become that far off distant past

Where the poetry of old
Was wrote from our souls
And I hope to write some of those that last

The Shot

With my back against a tree trunk
After scraping the dry leaves away
Sitting there in peaceful silence
Just before the break of day

The dark woods are all around me
But it is I, the night should fear
For I am here to take a life today
And to bring my family back a deer

Soon the morning birds are chirping
I see my breath each time I breathe
The sun has lit its golden candle
And it's getting light enough to see

My fourteen year old younger self
Was in his place of perfect bliss
His favorite rifle in his hands
The one in which he never missed

And when the ghost of the forest
Stepped out to feel the sun
I silently took the safety off
And then slowly raised my gun

Half a mile from our back door
This memory, I have not forgot
With a house full of hungry mouths
I held my breath and took the shot

Chapter Two:
Difficult Poetry to Write

A Trail I've Taken

A trail has split in an autumn wood
My rifle and I could not trod both
Hunting alone, I quietly stood
Staring down each as best I could
Till both faded into the undergrowth

There, my choice decides how well I'll fare
While eyes sought which best to claim
Each well trodden with plenty wear
Proof my prey was often there
But had not wore them both the same

The twain this morn before me lay
Where hooves of deer left marks of black
Then, I left one for some other day
The signs that lay, will show me the way
And if luck prevails I will not be back

A forlorn tale ends with a sigh
Yet joy, this one forever hence
A trail split in an autumn wood, and I
I chose the one more trodden by
That choice had made all the difference.

The hardest words to rhyme

Bastard
The old cowboy handed me an orange
As we looked out across his Bar range
On a ranch, where I'd been working almost a month.

He had a thieving horse named, Silver
Who'd steal anything that he could pilfer
As we sat right there and had ourselves some lunch.

All his scarfs were colored purple
And he laughed just like Steve Urkel
And in his fancy vest, he always kept himself a pint.

He trained his horse to stomp his hoof
And then he'd howl just like a wolf
And said, "Every since I was a pup, I've been defiant".

With his guns he was awful dangerous
And even though it all looked strange to us
He could shoot them both while keeping perfect rhythm

He could hit a target near or far
And said he twice shot up a bar
And was a local legend on how good he had got with them

He told me his mother was quite a woman
And was the only one who got to know him
That she'll be gone for ten long years on the ninth.

He said she never had a husband
But she felt sure his daddy loved him
And said he knew just what he was, and won't deny it.

Me

Me, Myself and I
had a good question.

So I said "Me,
what say you, of I"?

And Me said "I,
I see you as, Myself."

And Myself said,
"So do I."

Convictus

There's a Christian inside of me
Who's life had nowhere else to go
I thank the only God there be
And His Son who saved my soul

I don't believe in happenstance
I hope my pen will do him proud
His bludgeoning had took a chance
And as a servant, he has bowed

He'll wipe away all of their tears
And lighten up dark valleys shade
And they can reminisce for years
Nothing is there to be afraid

The Lambs Book of Life is his gate
Through Heavens streets we'll have a stroll
His death on the Cross sealed my fate
And can restore again my soul

a·be·ce·dar·i·an

A poem beginning with the ABC's
Became a challenge I just saw today.
Can the poet who lives inside of me
Describe all the things he would like to say?

Every other line ending with a rhyme?
For that is how the poet in me writes
Giving attention to the syllables
Having no more than ten is what he likes.

Inside each line will the poem flow free
Just enough til he makes it to the end?
Knowing someone will always check his work
Looking for how well his story will blend

Minutes tick by while he looks for a word
Nowhere as easy at it may have seemed
Only eleven more lines left to go
Perhaps success is only in a dream

Questions that he needs to find answers to
Reminds him of the times that he has failed
Success has many times eluded him
Today he is determined to prevail

Unlike every other thing in his life
Victory lies within this poets reach
Whatever the finished version reveals
Xerox copies may be printed to teach

You see I am one person with two names
Zebras have different stripes they can blame.

Double a·be·ce·dar·i·an

A mans life is often explained like a waltz
Before those who attend his eulogy
Choosing to tell a story so complex
Doubt fills the minds of those who really knew

Everyone remains silent throughout the improv
Friends and family often add to the menu
Great memories are shared with regret
Hearts are devoured standing at these coffins

In memories their pain is often made bear
Just to hear kind comments provides some tranq
Kindness to others often provides a closeup
Letting others share times from long ago

Most will sit and listen with no addition
No one needs to share their hearts museum
Only family can share in those things nonvocal
Pallbearers are often chosen from menfolk

Quietly the preacher known as 'brother K J'
Reminding me of a picture of a sad faced emoji
Sits down while sad music causes tears to wash
This is the saddest part that's most foreboding

Understanding and joining in with tears of grief
Videos often play filled with a favorite picture
We are reminded once again of the grace of GOD
Xerox copied pamphlets records these things historic

You gather at the place where dirt will entomb
Zillions of heavens rewarded will say Aloha

Chapter Three: Addiction

Addiction

My name is called "Addiction"
And I want to be your friend
And have a good time while we're together
And tomorrow it can end.

I come in many flavors
Each is yours to freely choose
Try me only for amusement
What have you got to lose?

And when you taste my precious venom
I'll become the one that you adore
And you'll come back to me just one more time
For more and more and more.

Your friends will no longer matter
Your family put to the test
I see the bad that hides inside
They only see the best.

I will destroy what you hold sacred
I will defile what you hold dear
Any self-respect that you have left
I will make it disappear.

I only have one weakness
And that is your "Willingness to Fight"
Will it be a minor skirmish
Or a War with All Your Might?

And if somehow I am defeated
And your willingness prevails
I will take you back with open arms
And I will put your life through Hell!

THE WOLF

ADDICTION IS A WOLF, OUT LOOKING FOR PREY
HE CIRCLES THE HERD, IN SEARCH OF A STRAY
HE FEEDS ON THE OLD, THE YOUNG, AND THE WEAK
IN SEARCH OF A VICTIM, HE CAN EASILY DEFEAT ...

THE BULL THINKS HE'S TOUGH, AND CAN PUT UP A FIGHT
AND ONE DAY HIS OWN HERD, IS NO LONGER IN SIGHT
THE YEARS HE HAS SPENT, HAD BECOME QUITE A BORE
SO HE STRAYED FAR AWAY, WHILE SEARCHING FOR MORE ...

THE NOSE OF THE WOLF, HAD THEN GOTTEN HIS SCENT
AND COULD TELL BY THE SMELL, WHERE HIS TIME HAD BEEN SPENT
JUST LIKE THE OTHERS WHO HAD PROVIDED A FEAST
HE REEKED FROM THE SMELL, THAT HIS SINS HAD RELEASED ...

ALL THE MUCK AND THE MIRE, FROM WHERE HE HAD BEEN
CAUSED THE JUICES TO DRIP, FROM HIS JAWS, WITH A GRIN
THE PACK WHOM HE SUMMONED, SOON CIRCLED AROUND
BUT A BULL WHO WAS WEAK, IS WHAT THEY HAD FOUND ...

IT DIDN'T TAKE LONG, UNTIL HE WAS UNDER ATTACK
THE STRENGTH OF THE HERD, WAS SOMETHING HE LACKED
HE WAS ALL ON HIS OWN, FOR THEY WERE TOO FAR AWAY
AND THE PRICE FOR HIS SINS, WOULD HAVE TO BE PAID ...

HE FOUGHT TO GO HOME, AS THEY RIPPED AT HIS FLESH
AND HE LONGED FOR THE LIFE HE WOULD LOVE TO REFRESH
HE WAS WOUNDED AND BATTERED, BUT STILL ON HIS FEET
THE HERD'S JUST AHEAD, AND WILL END HIS DEFEAT ...

AND WHEN HE FINALLY ARRIVED, MORE DEAD THAN ALIVE
SO FILLED WITH SHAME, FROM THE LOOK IN THEIR EYES
FOR ONCE AGAIN, HE RETURNED, SO TIRED HE COLLAPSED
WITH ONE MORE EXCUSE, WHY AGAIN HE RELAPSED ...

AND THEN HE JOINED IN THE HERD, AND AGAIN HE WOULD HEAL
BUT HIS EYES SOUGHT THE FUN, THAT WAS JUST OVER THE HILL
AND THE WOLF LIES IN WAIT, UNTIL THE DAY HE RETURNS
BECAUSE THE BULL IS TOO STUBBORN, AND UNWILLING TO LEARN ...

AND HIS HERD ALL LOVES HIM, BUT THEY HAVE TO MOVE ON
AND PRAY THAT THE NEXT TIME, HE'LL MAKE IT BACK HOME
UNTIL THE TIME COMES, HE'S FINALLY CHOSEN TO STAY
OR BECOMES A BIG PILE OF DUNG, OUT THERE WASTING AWAY ...

Quitting Meth

I quit Meth about a month ago
And I quit again last week
And I may quit again tomorrow
With a new improved technique.

Or I will quit when there's no sorrow
Or I will quit when there's no pain
And I will quit this time 'for certain'
When there's no one else to blame.

Then I will get back what Meth has taken
And replace all that it cost
And I will mend all that's been broken
And restore all that I've lost.

Just one last time again 'I promise'
And I will quit this time for sure
Or maybe, after another
Now that I've found the cure.

The Devil In Me

There is a devil who lives inside of me
Whom I fed one fateful day,
Where he found himself a place to live
And decided he would stay

I let him starve a time or two
To show him whose the boss,
But I fed this devil inside of me
And it was I who paid the cost

First he took away my dignity
Where I've done things which I abhor,
But I kept feeding this devil inside of me
And he always wanted more

There was not a line I would not cross
No price I wouldn't pay,
I just fed the devil inside of me
And let him have his way

Weeks turned into months and then
Those months turned into years,
The devil who lives inside of me
Had filled my life with tears

But I finally reached rock bottom
And decided I need a change,
So I quit feeding the devil inside of me
Now my life is rearranged

But he still lives there, deep inside
Just waiting to be fed,
But I will starve this devil inside of me
Until either he or I am dead

Chapter Four:
Funeral Poems

Momma's "Dash"

When I saw her picture in the paper
Beside the others who had passed
I had to stop there for a little while
And take a look at "momma's dash"

That little line between her birthday
And the date when she was gone
Holds the memories of a lifetime
That she had spent to make a home

It holds every hug that she hand given
And every cheek that she had kissed
And all the worries of a mother
With all the sleep that she had missed

It holds all the good times I remember
And all the Bad, that I recall
And now that little dash, so unimportant
Means So Much now, after all

It holds the sound of her voice singing
And those times when she had wept
And all those prayers she prayed to Jesus
On those nights before she slept

And now that little dash between her birthday
And the date, when she was gone
Is replaced by God's eternal dash
That goes on and on and on...

A Day

Floating on a gentle breeze
A slip of paper caught my stare
I glanced to find from wince it came
But no one else was there

Descending ever slowly
Dancing round from east to west
But the moment I reached out my hand
That's where it came to rest

It was a letter old and faded
Without a single crease or tear
Let loose upon a journey
For the wind alone to bare

A message sent from heaven?
From a loved one, some might say
To give a glimpse of what it's like
To be there for a day

It read,

"A day is like a thousand days
And ten thousand days, just one
For when a thousand days have ended there
A day here, just begun

No one is in a hurry
And His Glory lights the sky,
And before you even realize
Ten thousand days passed by"

That's when I thought of all my loved ones lost
Some of whom, for many years
That time no longer means a thing
And have nothing left to fear

So I opened up my hand that day
And sent this letter on its way
For I know that we will meet again
If it takes forever, or a day

Hello

We are here today to say goodbye
With our family and our friends,
To mourn the loss of one we love
But this is not the end

Although all of us will miss you
This Christian family knows,
That while we are here to say goodbye
Jesus Christ has said hello

"For to be absent from this life" Paul said
"Is to be present, with the Lord",
Still those of us, who love you most
Have found this awful hard

But from the moment in which you left us
You were placed in his embrace,
And for accepting him as Savior
Your reward for this is Grace

"For eye has not seen, nor ear has heard
The things he has in store ..."
We know that you are with him now
In a place with so much more

A "New Life" has been given you
He has restored again your soul,
And Forever you will be with him
When you heard him say "Hello"

A Songbirds Dream

In the early morning hour
with the warmth the sunlight brings,
Awakes the tiny songbird
with a song he has to sing

For while he slept in peaceful slumber
He dreamt a dream, so fair,
Now there's nothing more important
than this dream he has to share

So perched high upon a treetop
Before all that he beholds,
He sings aloud, this song he has
in words an angel knows

And what is this song of wonder
that he awoke today to sing ?
Well it seems a child of God, he knew
Has received, their set of wings

Why?

How do I overcome this sadness
Or begin to say goodbye?
Where do I go to find the answers
So I can understand the reason Why?

Like Christ I felt forsaken
The day you took my son away
Lord, why did our prayers go unanswered
When so many people prayed?

I cried out to you in anger
And begged to let me take his place
Oh how I long to hear his voice again
And to see his smiling face

But you controlled the dawn of all creation
And laid the foundations of the earth
And it was You who gave "The breath of life"
And the miracle of birth

So who am I, that I should question
The choice you made that day?
For "It is the Lord who giveth,
And the Lord who takes away"

But there is a thought where I find comfort
And in my heart I know it's true
And that is, You took my son away from me
So he can spend more time with You

Torn In Two

On the day I had to say goodbye
My soul was torn in two
Where a piece of it stayed here with me
But the rest went there with you

It's a part of me I can't get back
So for now it's just on loan
So keep it close to you until
The good Lord calls me home

Then you can give back that part of me
And I'll give back my piece of you
And never will that part of us
Be torn again in two

My Love For You (Alzheimer's)

When my memory of us has faded,
And I can no longer recognize.
And you see, the love we shared together,
Is no longer in my eyes.

When my stare is filled with emptiness,
And my speech is all but gone.
It is time for you to say goodbye,
And The Lord to call me home.

And when our friends have come together,
And have shown their last respects.
There is still one thing I ask of you,
And out of love, I will expect.

Do not mourn too long my passing,
And find new joy in all you do.
Not because of your love for me,
But for the love I have for you.

Do not stand at my grave and cry

Do not stand at my grave and cry
Do not come here to say goodbye
My time on earth I spent with you
This gift God gave, was my gift to

Now comes the greatest gift of all
Gods gift of grace, and Satan's fall
Eternal Life by Christs own hands
Heaven and earth is his command

Though it may take us a little while
Till we embrace and share a smile
To receive this gift it's plain to see
"This mortal shall put on immortality"

And when my gift of God has come
For I have accepted His only Son
Do not come here to say goodbye
Do not stand at my grave and cry

Glory

On the day in which you left us
I heard an angel cry,
And beheld a thousand hosts of heaven
Who were proudly standing by

There appeared a Mighty Cherub
Who read a great decree,

"Go And Seek Out My Faithful Servant.
And Bring Him Here To Me"

Michael's army prepared for battle
To defend this noble cause,
For this child of God who kept the faith
And walked in all his laws

A Chariot stood waiting
With Honor Guards galore,
And thus began your trip to GLORY
Who could ask for any more?

The Kingdom

In Gods Kingdom there is a river
And the "Tree of Life" is there,
Its leaves are for the healing
For the dwellers there to share

I will meet you beside that river
And share a drink or two,
And take a bite from the Tree of Life
And give a piece to you

"In my fathers house, there are many mansions"
We could visit every one,
And walk throughout his Kingdom
Watching children having fun

Our friendship has not ended
For all eternity lies ahead,
"The gift of God is eternal life"
Is what his word has said

No Dispute

She stood outside Gods gardens gate
As many souls had also done
Her sins washed by the lambs blood
And now her change had come

The flaming sword held its peace
And His cherub led the way
All the days of her appointed time
Where mortals cannot stay

The tree of life lie just ahead
Its branches heavy with its fruit
The gift of God is eternal life
And hers is no longer in dispute

Goodbye

Goodbye is not forever
It's to only wish you well
Memories you have left me with
Are both of ours to tell

Parting may bring us sorrow
Till the morrow when we meet
Where the joy of reuniting
Makes the waiting awful sweet

I can feel my heart is aching
And the sadness will have a try
But I know it's not forever
So for now it's just goodbye

Jacob's Ladder

I dreamed I ascended Jacobs Ladder
Where God's angels come and go,
And saw the earth in all its beauty
Disappearing far below

And when I reached the Gates of Glory
And Saint Peter asked me "Why"?
I said "I come to ask the question,
Why do little children die"?

Then I heard the sound of thunder
At these words that I had said,
And saw a multitude of angels
As they knelled, and bowed their heads

Then standing there before me
As I shook at what I saw,
There stood Alpha and Omega
The Creator of us all

His hair appeared as lightning
With eyes brighter than the sun,
And was accompanied by cherubs
From wherever He had come

And in this dream of mine, so vivid
He reached out to me, His hand,
And He who brought forth all creation
Appeared before me, as a man

Then He spoke of things I cannot mention
And said those things I cannot say,
As we walked throughout His Kingdom
Watching little children play

And when this day was almost over
And each were carried off to bed,
He smiled at this a moment
Then turned to me and said

"Free will, to all is given
Before Eternal Life will come,
And each will prove if he is worthy
But these are those in need of none"

And as I descended Jacob's Ladder
I thought of all that He had said,
And how the death of little children
Becomes Eternal Life instead

A Quarter On A Tombstone

He placed a quarter on the tombstone
Then he knelt down in the grass,
Where he read every word written
About this memory from the past.

Some had left a penny
Others had left a dime,
Some took a nickel from their pocket
That could take them back in time.

But this one paid a quarter
To see this soldier who was lost
For he watched the angel take his soul
And Jesus smiled, and paid the cost

Heaven Needs Children Too

When heavens realm had been created
All the angels gathered round,
And beheld its awesome wonders
Nothing lacking they had found

God Almighty stood in silence
For in His heart He knew,
What kind of place would heaven be
Without some children too?

Only for a moment
He considered what must be done,
Then His cherubim were summoned
The joy of heaven had begun

Grandparents for generations
Countless mothers throughout the years,
All adoring laughing children
As the angels brought them here

Every heart is filled with kindness
For this innocence so pure,
Christ the Lord abiding with them
Their salvation is secure

From the first child received by angels
Heavens population grew,
For what kind of place would heaven be
Without some children too?

Chapter Five: What Makes A Poem

Poetry Tip

Get their attention early
Or you've waited too long,
A well written poem
Flows just like a song

If in need of a rhyme
Maybe find another word,
One that is forced
Is the loudest one heard

Then pick it all over
And pick it apart once again,
Once it's been put out there
You may not can reel it back in

Poetry Tip 11

I will share with you some wisdom from some things I have learned
That the poet who is inside me will neither deny or confirm
First we write out a sentence that is making the point
And the second line is where we'd try to use the rhyming word 'joint'

It cuts down half your rhyming while you're trying to write
And in that single line wide open you can paint the world bright
Then sew them both together in some words using wit
It's the second line that's hardest always giving me fits

But when it's finally over and you pause and go back
Take out all the flaws but leave your message intact
So many poems are wasted and their meanings are lost
When every "I" has been dotted and every "T" has been crossed

Poetry Tip III

If you want to write a poem write a poem not a book
And spend a little time on the way that it looks
Separate the stanza's, so they're easy to read
Then some worthy subject matter is all you'll need

The first couple of lines, will decide the poems fate
Will it be mediocre, or will it be great?
Through the eyes of the writer is what we will see
Whatever you've written down, is what it will be

Choose your words wisely, so that the story will flow
When it's not written correctly, how else will we know?
Just what was 'the point', you were trying to make?
And to let a poem 'ramble', is a common mistake

Whether you're a poet master, or a poet laureate
These are some things you should never forget
Poetry is an art, to try and find the right words
And any that are forced, are the loudest ones heard

Whataburger

In the early morning hour
Or like a beacon late at night,
Those orange and white colors
Have become a welcome sight

Chicken strips, toast and gravy
Or a double meat with cheese,
With, or without onions
Just anyway you please

Where old folks meet for breakfast
And teenagers late at night,
Whataburger is a 24/7 kind of place
That makes you feel just right

Whataburger (Poem #2)

My morning starts with coffee
And a breakfast on a bun
With bacon, eggs or sausage
I have tried them every one

Hashbrown sticks and ketchup
A breakfast platter, has it all
Pancakes or Taquito's
With an orange juice, large or small

A mushroom, Swiss cheese burger
An all time favorite at noon
Then "Whatasize" that Whataburger
And you'll come back again ...real soon

About the Author Lonnie Budro

Lonnie was born and raised in an area known as "The Big Thicket", in Southeast Texas.

Born in the town of Liberty, in the mid 1960's. He grew up in the nearby small towns of Batson, and Saratoga Texas, where he attended, and graduated West Hardin Independent School District, in Saratoga in 1983.

Lonnie discovered a natural gift, at writing poetry much later in life after the death of his father in 2007.

He currently has written over 300 poems, recorded several songs, and is in the process of publishing some of his work, including a couple of children's books, now that he has become a grandfather.

About the Artist Jessica Budro

Jessica Budro is an aspiring artist from East Texas who has been creating art since childhood. From simple doodles to progressively exploring other mediums, Jessica is looking to find her niche. She has explored sketching, colored pencils, watercolor, and acrylic paints, as well as digital art and continues to learn more.

www.ingramcontent.com/pod-product-compliance
Lightning Source LLC
Chambersburg PA
CBHW071855070526
44583CB00016B/1698